This book is intended
to spark conversations about empathy,
differences, and self-compassion.

Through the text children will learn not
only about **Type 1 Diabetes** but also about the
diversity of people who are living bravely with
T1D. The book is perfect for newly diagnosed
children, siblings, and classrooms that have a
student living with T1D.

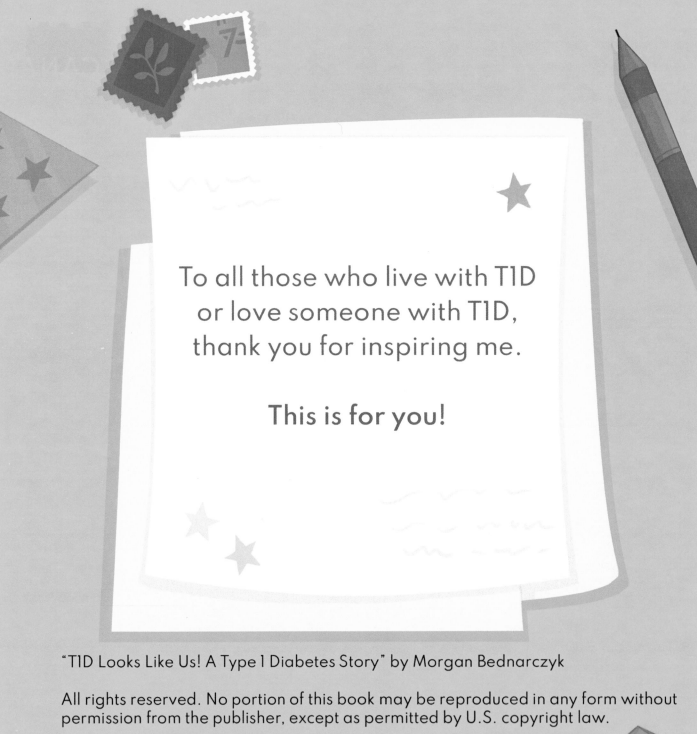

To all those who live with T1D
or love someone with T1D,
thank you for inspiring me.

This is for you!

"T1D Looks Like Us! A Type 1 Diabetes Story" by Morgan Bednarczyk

Copyright © 2022 by Morgan Bednarczyk
Illustrated by Hayley Moore

ISBN: 978-0-578-29700-2 (paperback)

First Edition

T1D
LOOKS LIKE US!
A Type 1 Diabetes Story

Morgan Bednarczyk

illustrated by **Hayley Moore**

POSTAGE STAMP

My name is Rose. I am nine years old and in the fourth grade. I love drawing and playing with my cat, Dexter.

I also have **Type 1 Diabetes**, sometimes called **T1D** for short, but that is not something I like to tell people about all the time.

In the summer when I was seven years old, I wanted to sleep with a water bottle in bed because I was so thirsty.

I would also wake up in the middle of the night with soggy sheets from wetting the bed. I was so embarrassed that sometimes I did not tell my parents until the morning.

My mom took me to the doctor, and after hearing my symptoms and noticing that I had lost a lot of weight, a nurse poked my finger to use some of my blood to run a test.

When the doctor came back into the room, he told my mom that I had Type 1 Diabetes and my **blood sugar** was way too high. I had no idea what that was and tightly held Mom's hand.

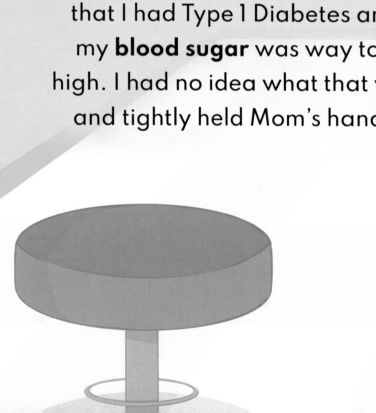

DIABETES

The pancreas creates insulin. Insulin helps glucose get into your cells.

The stomach turns food into glucose.

We were sent to the hospital for a few nights to learn about Type 1 Diabetes. The diabetes educator, Emily, taught me that in our bodies we all have a **pancreas** that makes insulin.

Insulin helps our bodies maintain energy so we can learn and play. My pancreas stopped making insulin and that made my blood sugar too high.

Now I have to get injections of insulin to keep my blood sugar steady. Emily taught my mom and I how to give me insulin shots. She even brought me an orange to practice on until I was able to do it to myself.

Before I take insulin,
I have to check my blood sugar
so that I take the correct amount of insulin.
I poke my finger several times a day. I place
a small amount of blood on a paper strip
in a machine and it gives me a number.

This number is used to determine how much insulin I need to take if it is too high or if I need a snack because it is too low.

My favorite things to have when my sugar is low are juice boxes and fruit snacks.

I have to get insulin when my blood sugar is high and when I eat. All foods have **carbohydrates** in them, and the more carbohydrates I eat, the more insulin my body needs.

Even though I have to monitor my food, I can still eat what I enjoy in healthy portions! My parents help me count my carbs so I get the right amount of insulin.

After getting used to taking shots, I was able to get an **insulin pump**. It is a little device that looks like a phone that is connected to my body with a tube. When I eat food, I tell the pump how many carbs I ate, and it sends the insulin into me through the tube.

At my school I am the only person with Type 1 Diabetes, and that makes me feel lonely sometimes. Some people stare at me when I have to get insulin or whisper to each other when I am checking my blood sugar.

My dad taught me that sometimes people do that because they do not understand what life with diabetes is like. My mom has helped me make friends with others who have diabetes around the world.

Zoey is ten years old and has had diabetes since she was five. She tried an insulin pump but decided she would rather do shots.

Even though Zoey has diabetes and uses a wheelchair, it doesn't stop her from her dream of being an artist!

Zoey wears a device on her body called a Continuous Glucose Monitor (**CGM**).

The CGM sends her blood sugar levels to her parents' phones so she does not need to poke her finger as much. If her blood sugar dips too low while she is sleeping, Zoey's parents bring her juice. Zoey's special talent is drinking juice in her sleep to get her sugar up!

Liam is six and lives in London, England. He loves to play chess and bake with his mom. Liam and his mom have a special bond. Liam's mom also has diabetes! Together, they are experts at counting the carbohydrates in their cookies.

When Liam got sick when he was little, his mom recognized the symptoms, and he was also diagnosed with Type 1 Diabetes. The family has a dog called Daisy who is trained to detect when Liam or his mom has high or low blood sugar.

Far away in Uganda, **Amos** lives with his mom and grandparents. He has Type 1 Diabetes too!

Amos and his mother have to walk a long way to get to the doctor's office. It is sometimes difficult for him to get the supplies he needs to live.

Amos does not let his T1D set him back. His family members work hard to help him get the medication he needs to keep him safe and well. He still enjoys playing football with his neighborhood friends.

They watch out for him and take a break if he needs water or something to eat.

Grace is a grown-up who has Type 1 Diabetes. She is friends with my mom. She has had diabetes for over thirty years! That is a very long time.

Grace worked hard to have her dream job as a writer, got married, and moved far away from home in the United States to live in Australia. Diabetes never stopped her from following her heart.

With help from doctors, family, and friends, Grace is a mom to two little boys. She loves playing with them on the playground and riding bikes. The kids always like to carry fruit snacks in their pockets in case their mom needs to treat low blood sugar.

Learning about other people living with diabetes has made me feel less alone. My mom has helped me meet others with diabetes on the internet and in person.

I am pen pals with Zoey and we enjoy writing letters and sending mail back and forth to encourage each other.

Even though I cannot be around these people whenever I want, just knowing they are there makes me feel less alone!

ABOUT THE AUTHOR

Morgan Bednarczyk,
M.S.Ed., LPC, is a licensed
professional counselor who
specializes in working with
children and adolescents.

She was diagnosed with
Type 1 Diabetes at the age
of seventeen. Five years
after her diagnosis, Morgan attended an
annual Children with Diabetes Friends for Life
conference in Orlando, Florida.

Her experiences at this conference meeting
young children living with T1D truly inspired her.
Since then she has made it her life passion to
advocate and educate others about
Type 1 Diabetes.

ABOUT THE ARTIST

Hayley Moore is a children's book illustrator and character designer on a mission to bring more empathy, diversity and light to today's kids.

With a sense of childlike wonder and a love for all things whimsical, she found her calling early in the colorful world of kids content.

When Hayley isn't doodling she is often found reading, forgetting to water her plants then desperately trying to revive them, using too many exclamation marks, and eating large amounts of Ben & Jerry's.

hayleysdoodles.com

To Parents of Children with Diabetes:

Use this book to explore your child's fears related to diabetes. Allow them to ask questions as they discover both the joys and hardships of life with T1D.

This book provides a look at different ways to manage T1D, giving readers an opportunity to learn about how others live and making space for children to explore different modes of T1D management they may be interested in trying.

When living with Type 1 Diabetes, having a choice is one of the biggest freedoms, and I hope to share that message within the pages of this book.